UKE 'AN PLAY
LED ZEPPELIN

MW00812100

Produced by
Alfred Music Publishing Co., Inc.
P.O. Box 10003
Van Nuys, CA 91410-0003
alfred.com

Printed in USA.

ISBN-10: 0-7390-9141-7
ISBN-13: 978-0-7390-9141-8

Cover photo: Photofest

CONTENTS

BLACK DOG

Words and Music by
JIMMY PAGE, ROBERT PLANT
and JOHN PAUL JONES

Black Dog - 5 - 1

walk that   way,___ watch your hon - ey   drip,___ can't   keep   a - way._____

E5

A5

A5

Oh___

Chorus:

C5

A5

___ yeah,   oh____ yeah,   ah____   ah____   ah.__

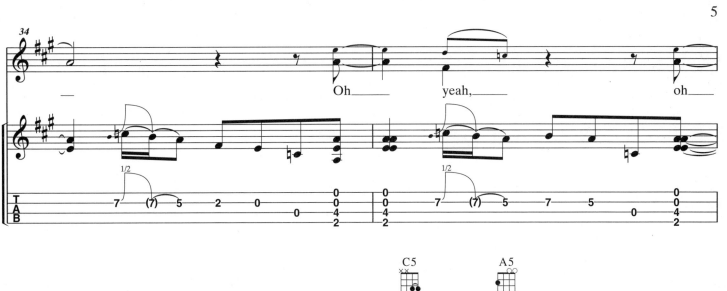

Verses 2 & 4:

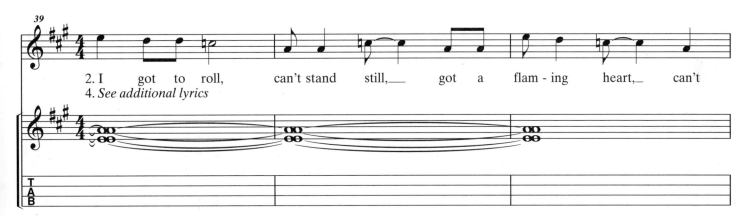

Eyes that shine,__ burn-ing red,__ dreams of you__ all

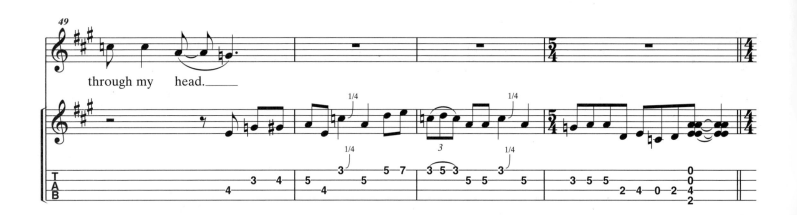

through my head._____

Ah ah ah ah ah ah ah ah

To Coda

A5

ah ah ah ah ah._____ Hey,__

Bridge:

C5 A5 G5

__ ba-by, oh__ ba-by, pret-ty ba-by, { dar-ling,
{ move me

BABE I'M GONNA LEAVE YOU

Words and Music by
ANNE BREDON, JIMMY PAGE
and ROBERT PLANT

Babe I'm Gonna Leave You - 6 - 1

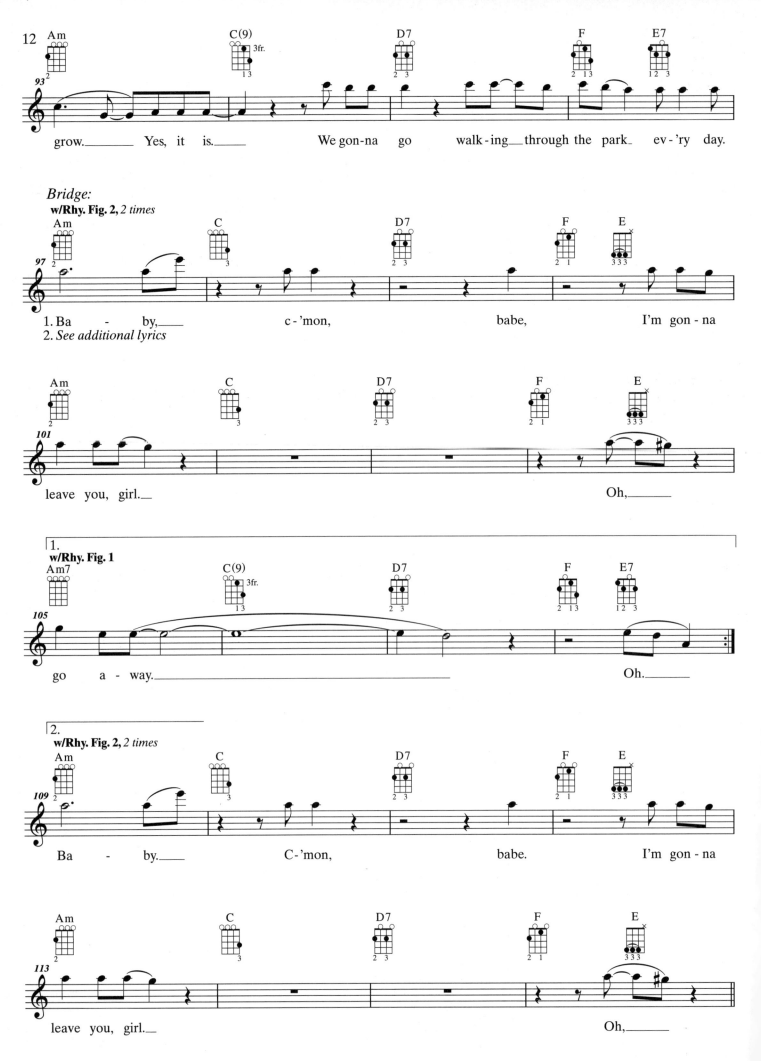

Verse 2:
Babe, babe, babe, babe, babe, babe, baby,
Mmm, baby, I wanna leave you,
I ain't joking, woman, I've got to ramble.
I can hear it calling me the way it used to do.
I can hear it calling me back home.
(To Bridge:)

Verse 3:
I know, I know, I know I'm never, never, never, never,
Never gonna leave you, babe.
But I got to go away from this place.
I got to quit you, yeah.
Oh, baby, baby, baby, baby.
(To Bridge:)

Verse 5:
Oh, miss your lips, sweet baby.
It was really, really good.
You made me happy ev'ry single day.
But now I've got to go away.
Baby, baby, baby, baby.
(To Outro:)

COMMUNICATION BREAKDOWN

Words and Music by
JIMMY PAGE, JOHN PAUL JONES
and JOHN BONHAM

Play 4 times

1. Hey, girl,___ stop what you're do - ing.___
2. *See additional lyrics*

Hey,_____ girl,_____ you drive me to ru - in.___ I don't__ know__ what it is I like__ a - bout you___ but I like it a lot._____ Won't__ __ you let__ me hold___ you, let me feel your lov - ing touch.___

Communication Breakdown - 4 - 1

DANCING DAYS

Words and Music by
JIMMY PAGE and ROBERT PLANT

Moderate rock ♩ = 116

Verses 1 & 3:

1. Danc-ing days are here___ a-gain,___ the sum-mer eve-nings grow.
3. *See additional lyrics*

I got my flow-er, I got___ my pow-er,

Dancing Days - 4 - 1

Interlude:

Guitar Solo:

Outro:

Verse 3:
You told your mama I'd get you home
But you didn't say I had no car.
I saw a lion, he was standing alone
With a tadpole in a jar.
(To Chorus:)

Verse 4:
Said, dancing days are here again
As the summer evenings grow.
You are my flower, you are my power,
You are my woman who knows.
(To Chorus:)

GOOD TIMES BAD TIMES

Words and Music by
JIMMY PAGE, JOHN PAUL JONES
and JOHN BONHAM

HOUSES OF THE HOLY

Words and Music by
JIMMY PAGE and ROBERT PLANT

Houses of the Holy - 4 - 1

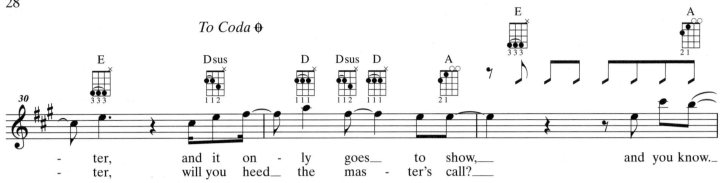

-ter, and it on - ly goes__ to show,__ and you know.__
-ter, will you heed__ the mas - ter's call?__

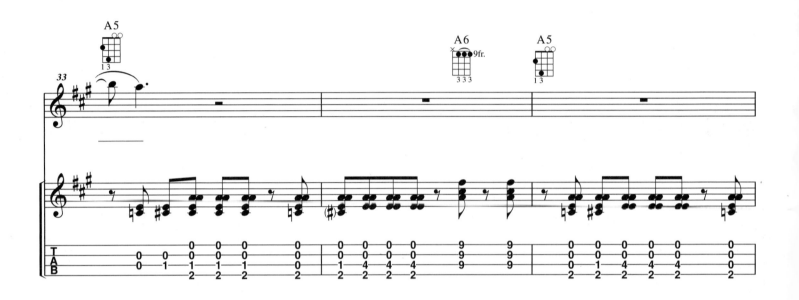

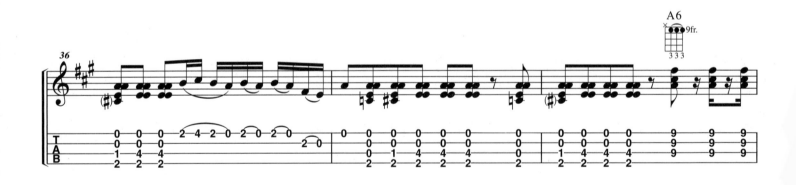

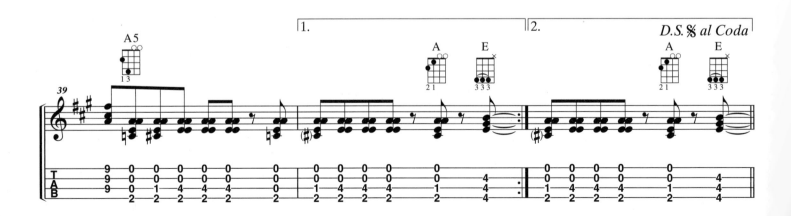

*Sung first time only.

Repeat and fade

Verse 3:
Said, there ain't no use in crying,
'Cause it will only, only drive you mad.
Does it hurt to hear them lying?
Was this the only world you had?
Oh. So let me take you to the movie,
Can I take you, baby, to the show?
Why don't you let me be yours ever truly?
Can I make your garden grow?
And you know that's right.

IMMIGRANT SONG

Words and Music by
JIMMY PAGE and ROBERT PLANT

Immigrant Song - 4 - 1

32

KASHMIR

Words and Music by
JIMMY PAGE, ROBERT PLANT
and JOHN PAUL JONES

Moderately slow ♩ = 80

Intro:

Kashmir - 6 - 1

Kashmir - 6 - 2

Bridge:

All   I   see   turns to

brown,_   as   the

sun   burns the   ground._

And   my   eyes___   fill with   sand,_

as   I   scan   this wast - ed land,_   try'n' to find,___

try'n' to find____   where I've   been._____

LIVING LOVING MAID
(She's Just a Woman)

Words and Music by
JIMMY PAGE and ROBERT PLANT

Fast rock ♩ = 152

Verses 1 & 3:

Cont. in notation

1. With a pur-ple um-brel-la and a fif-ty-cent hat,___
3. Tell-ing tall___ tales of how it used___ to be.___

(Liv-ing, lov-ing,

Cont. in notation

Mis-sus Cool rides___ out___ in her aged___ Cad-il-lac.
With the but-ler and the maid___ and the ser-vants three.___

she's just a wom-an)

Cont. in slashes

(Liv-ing, lov-ing, she's just a wom-an.

Cont. in slashes

Living Loving Maid (She's Just a Woman) - 4 - 1

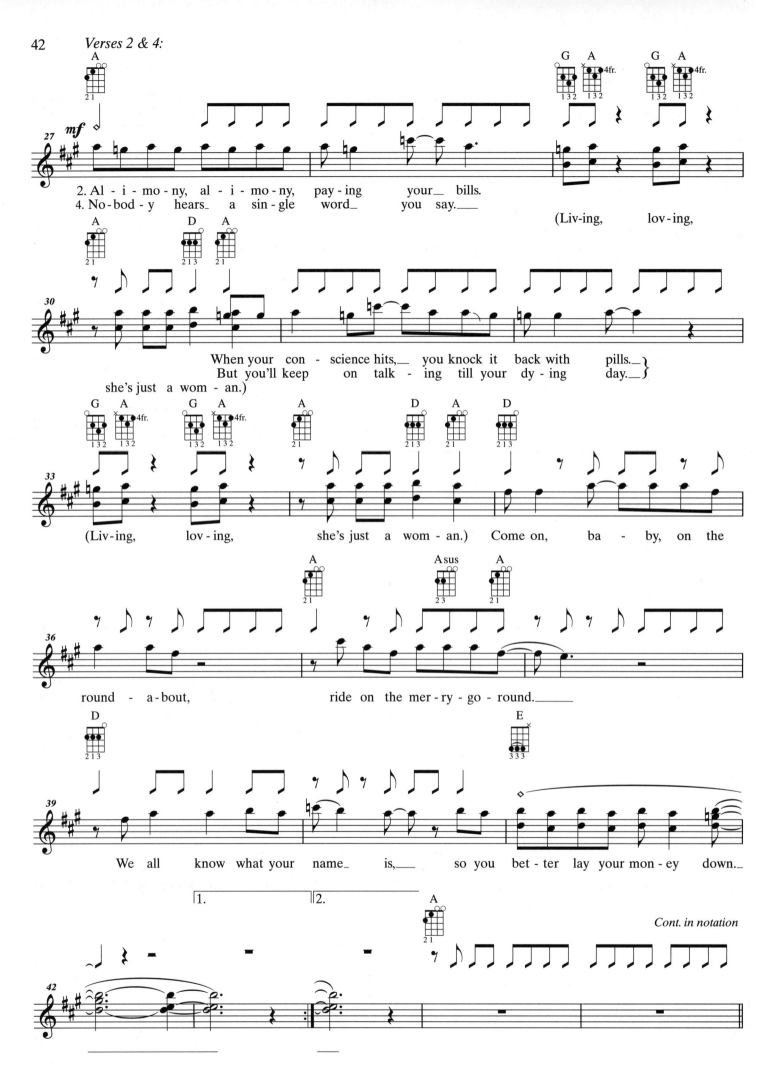

Living Loving Maid (She's Just a Woman) - 4 - 4

D'YER MAK'ER

Words and Music by
JIMMY PAGE, JOHN BONHAM,
JOHN PAUL JONES and ROBERT PLANT

D'yer Mak'er - 3 - 1

Verses 2, 4, & 6:

2. I,___ I, I, I, I, I,___ all those tears I cry,___ I, I, I,___ I.___
4. I,___ I, I, I, I, I,___ You hurt me to my soul.___ Oh, oh, oh,___ oh,___
6. See additional lyrics

___ all those___ tears I___ cry,___ oh,___ oh, I,
you hurt me to my soul.___ oh, oh,___

To Coda ⊕

I,___ ba - by, please_ don't go.___
oh.___ Dar - ling, please_ don't go.___

Bridge:

1. When I read the let-ter you wrote_ me,_ it made me mad, mad, mad._
2. When I read the let-ter you sent_ me,_ you made me mad, mad, mad._

Oh, when I___ read the words that it told_ me, it made me sad, sad, sad.
Oh, when I___ read the news that it brought_ me, it made me sad, sad, sad.

D'yer Mak'er - 3 - 2

IN THE EVENING

Words and Music by
JOHN PAUL JONES, JIMMY PAGE
and ROBERT PLANT

In the Evening - 5 - 1

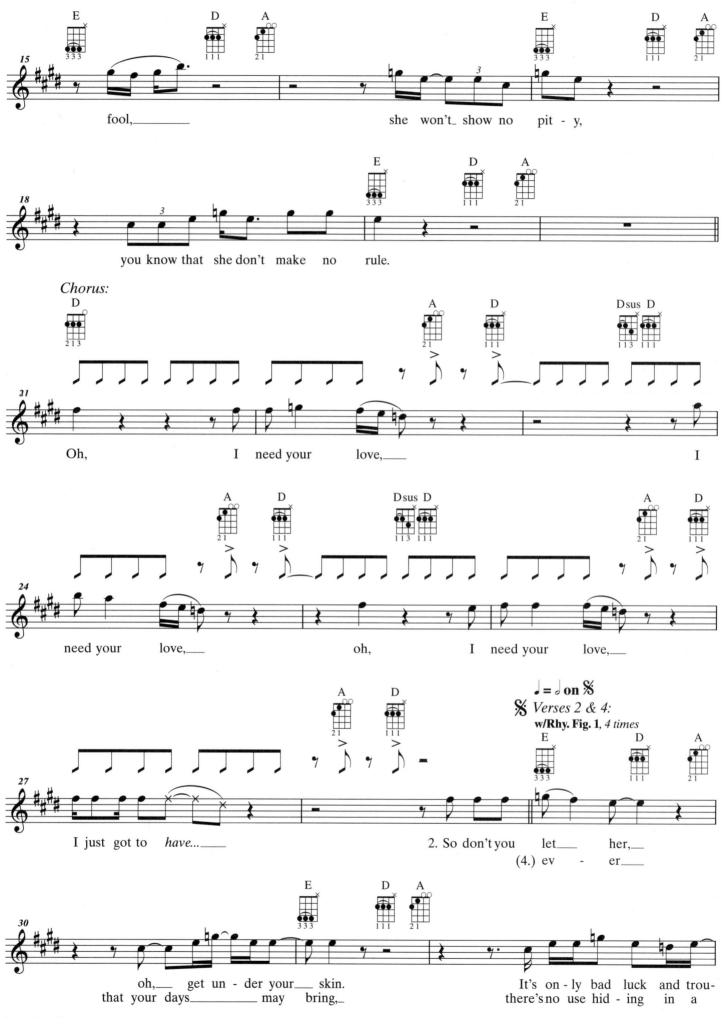

THE OCEAN

Words and Music by
JOHN BONHAM, JOHN PAUL JONES,
JIMMY PAGE and ROBERT PLANT

Moderately ♩ = 90

Intro:
Rhy. Fig. 1

end Rhy. Fig. 1

Verse:

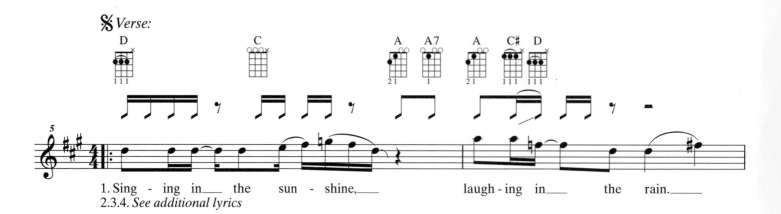

1. Sing - ing in___ the sun - shine,___ laugh - ing in___ the rain.___
2.3.4. *See additional lyrics*

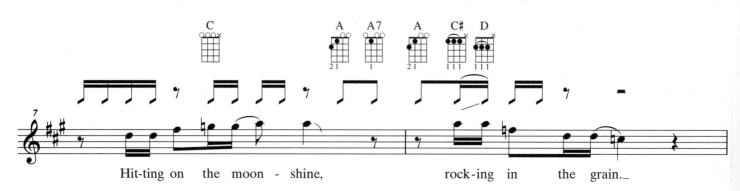

Hit-ting on the moon - shine, rock-ing in the grain.__

The Ocean - 4 - 1

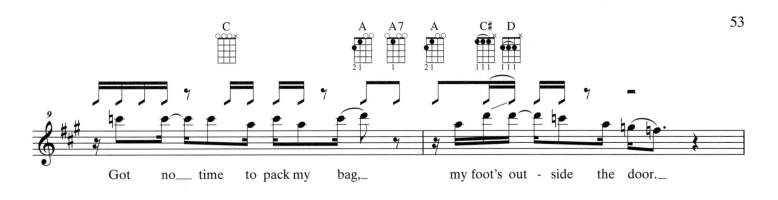

Got no__ time to pack my bag,__ my foot's out - side the door.__

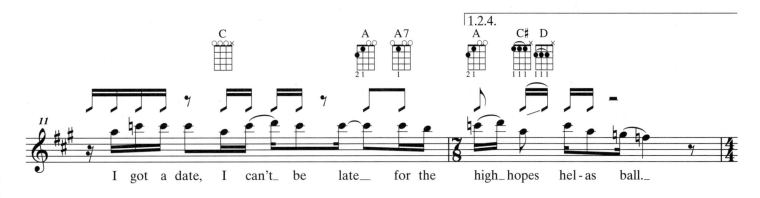

I got a date, I can't_ be late_ for the high_ hopes hel - as ball.__

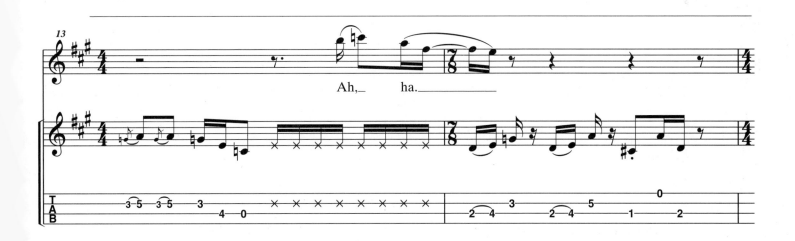

Ah,_ ha._____

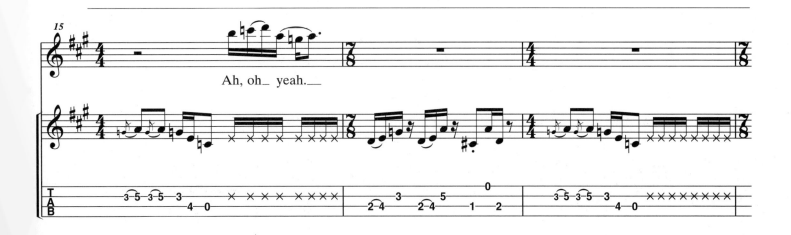

Ah, oh_ yeah.__

The Ocean - 4 - 2

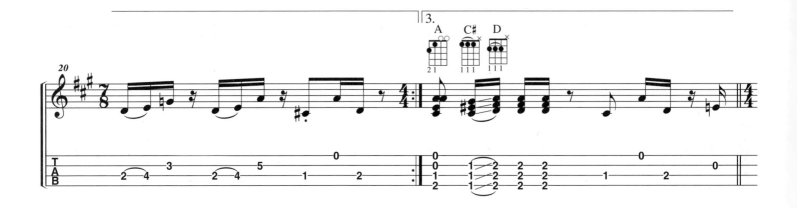

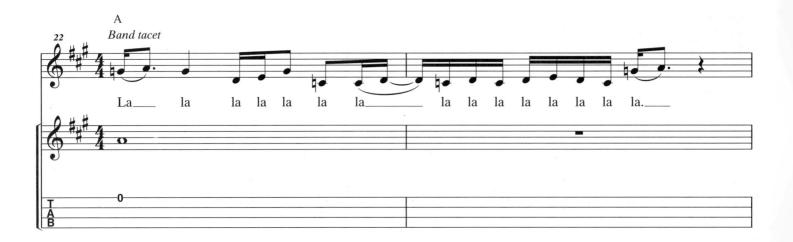

D.S. %Ñ al Coda

A,   yeah,_   yeah,_yeah!

Verse 2:
Singing to an ocean, I can hear the ocean's roar,
Play for free I play for me, I play a whole lot more.
Singing 'bout the good things, and the sun that lights the day,
I used to sing to the mountains, has the ocean lost its way?

Verse 3:
Instrumental

Verse 4:
Sitting 'round singing songs till the night turns into day,
Used to sing about mountains, but the mountains washed away.
Now I'm singing all my songs to the girl who won my heart,
She is only three years old, and it's a real fine way to start.

OVER THE HILLS AND FAR AWAY

Words and Music by
JIMMY PAGE and ROBERT PLANT

Moderate rock ♩ = 98

Intro:

Over the Hills and Far Away - 7 - 2

Play 5 times

Verses 5 & 6:
w/Rhy. Fig. 2

Mel-low is___ the man___ who knows what he's been miss - ing.
Man - y is___ a word___ that on - ly leaves you guess-ing,

Man - y, man - y men_____ can't see the o - pen road.___
guess - ing_____ 'bout a_____ thing___ you

ROCK AND ROLL

Words and Music by
JIMMY PAGE, ROBERT PLANT,
JOHN PAUL JONES and JOHN BONHAM

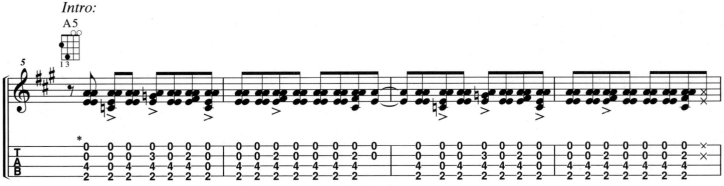

*Unison A notes played on 1st and 4th strings. See TAB for fingering.

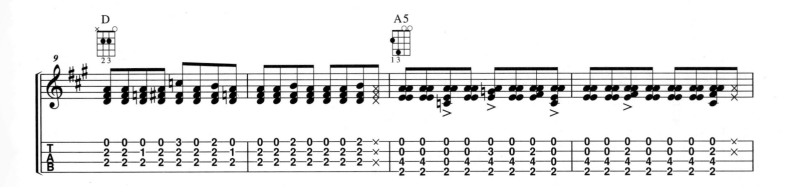

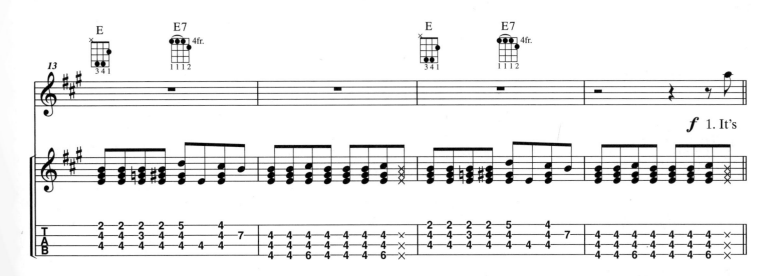

Rock and Roll - 5 - 1

Verse 3:
Instrumental

Verse 4:
It seems so long since we walked in the moonlight,
Making vows that just couldn't work right.
Open your arms, open your arms, open your arms
Baby, let my love come running in.
It's been a long time, been a long time,
Been a long, lonely, lonely, lonely, lonely, lonely time.

It's been a long time, been a long time,
Been a long, lonely, lonely, lonely, lonely, lonely time.

WHOLE LOTTA LOVE

*To play with original recording, tune Ukulele down one half step.

Moderately ♩ = 92

Words and Music by
JIMMY PAGE, ROBERT PLANT,
JOHN PAUL JONES, JOHN BONHAM
and WILLIE DIXON

*Recording sounds one half step lower than written.

Whole Lotta Love - 4 - 1

Chorus:

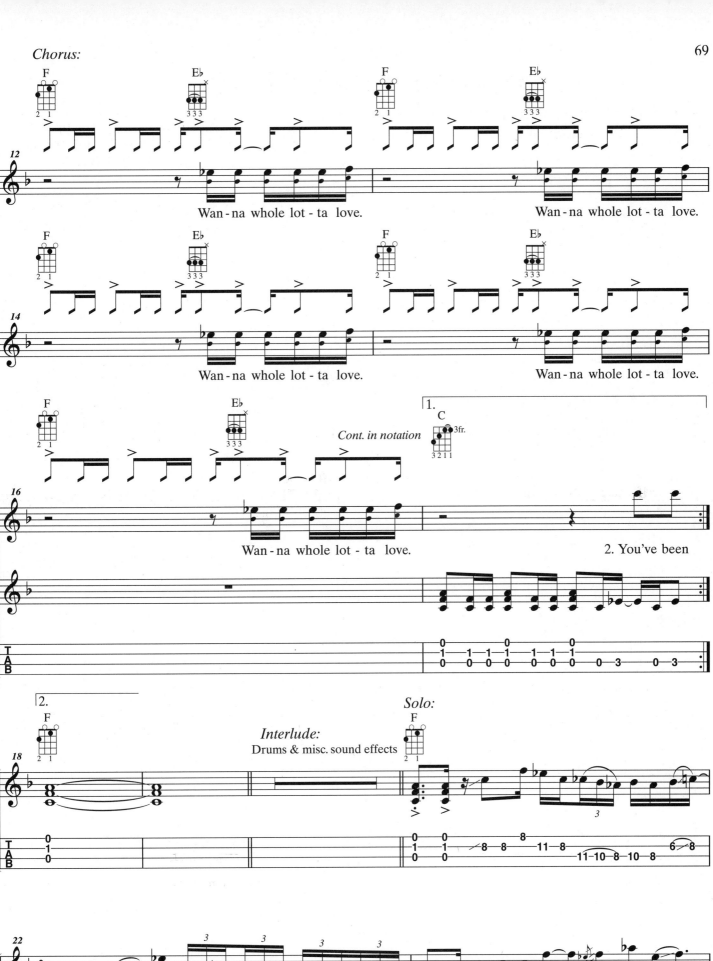

Wan - na whole lot - ta love.
Wan - na whole lot - ta love.

Wan - na whole lot - ta love.
Wan - na whole lot - ta love.

Cont. in notation

1.

Wan - na whole lot - ta love.

2. You've been

2.

Interlude:
Drums & misc. sound effects

Solo:

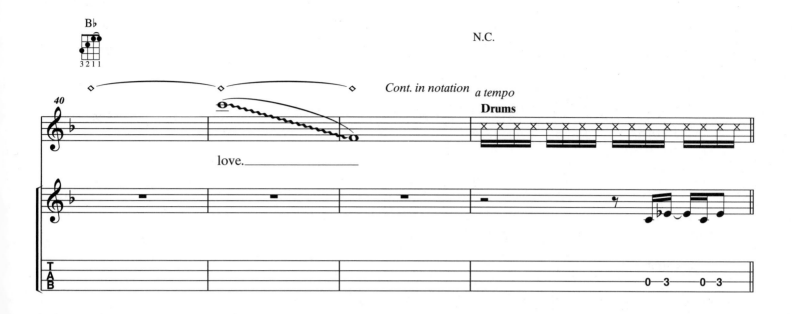

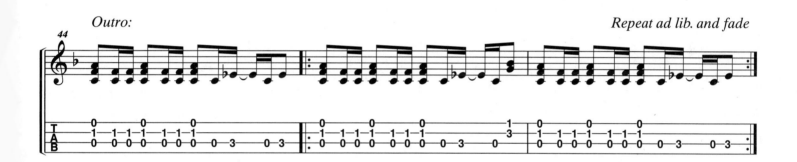

Verse 2:
You've been learning, and, baby, I been learning.
All them good times, baby, baby, I've been yearning.
Way, way down inside, honey, you need.
I'm gonna give you my love.
I'm gonna give you my love.
(To Chorus:)

Verse 3:
You've been cooling, and, baby, I've been drooling.
All the good times, baby, I've been misusing.
Way, way down inside, I'm gonna give you my love.
I'm gonna give you every inch of my love.
I'm gonna give you my love.
(To Chorus:)

STAIRWAY TO HEAVEN

Words and Music by
JIMMY PAGE and ROBERT PLANT

Stairway to Heaven - 9 - 1

74

Interlude:

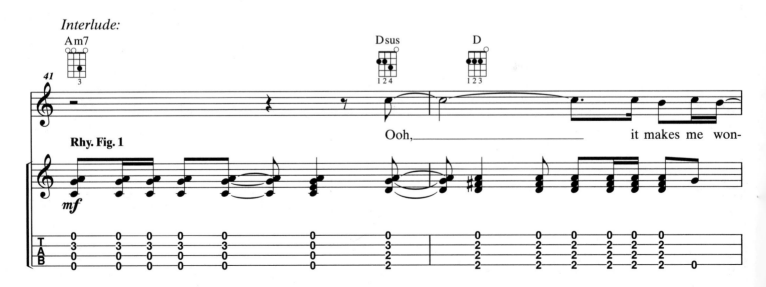

Stairway to Heaven - 9 - 3

C G Am
53
thoughts I have seen___ rings of smoke through the trees,___ and the
new day will dawn,___ for those who stand long,___ and the
C G F Am C G
55
voic - es of those who stand look - ing.
for - ests will ech - o with laugh - ter.
end Rhy. Fig. 1
w/Rhy. Fig. 1
Am7 Dsus D Am7 Em/D
58
(1st time only) Ooh,___ it makes me won - der.
D C/D D Am7 Dsus D
61
Ooh,___ it real - ly makes me won - der.
Am7 Em/D
1. D C/D D
2. D C/D D
64
3. And it's

Verses 4 & 5:

w/Rhy. Fig. 2

Band enters

4. If there's a bus-tle in your hedge-row, don't be a-larmed now,
5. Your head is hum-ming and it won't go, in case you don't know,

it's just a spring clean for the May___ Queen.
the pip-er's call-ing you to join___ him.

Yes, there are two paths you can go by, but in the long run,
Dear la-dy, can you hear the wind blow, and did you know,

there's still time to change_the road___ you're on.___
your stair-way lies on the___ whis-p'ring wind.___

1.

w/Rhy. Fig. 1

And it makes me won-der,

2.

◊ *Cont. in notation*

ahh.___

There walks a la - dy we all know,_____

who shines white light and wants to show,_____

Riff A - - - - - - - - - - - - - - - - - -
Elec. Gtr. *(arr. for uke)*

w/Riff A *3 times*

how ev - 'ry - thing___ still turns to gold._____

And if you lis - ten ver - y hard,_____

the tune will come to you___ at last._____

When all are   one__   and   one   is   all,_____

to   be   a   rock__   and   not   to   roll._____

And   she's   buy - ing   a   stair - way__   to   heav - en.__

UKE 'AN PLAY LED ZEPPELIN

UKULELE CHORD FRAME GLOSSARY

A CHORDS

A
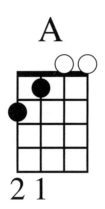
2 1

A
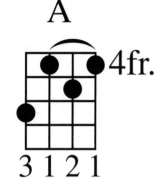
4fr.
3 1 2 1

Amaj7
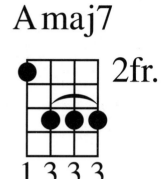
2fr.
1 3 3 3

A6
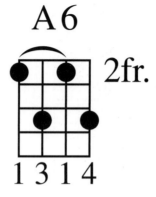
2fr.
1 3 1 4

Am
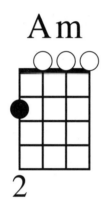
2

Am
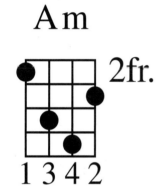
2fr.
1 3 4 2

Am7
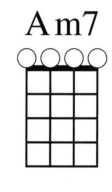

Am6
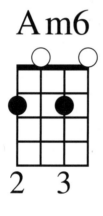
2   3

A7
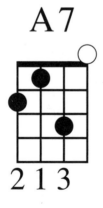
2 1 3

A7
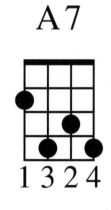
1 3 2 4

A9
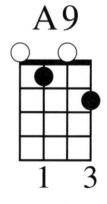
1   3

A13
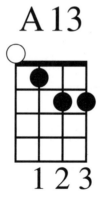
1 2 3

Asus
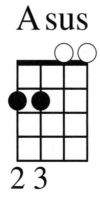
2 3

A7sus
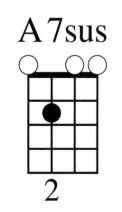
2

Adim7
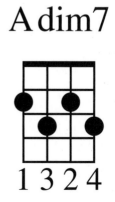
1 3 2 4

A+
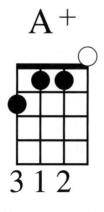
3 1 2

B♭ (A♯) CHORDS*

B♭
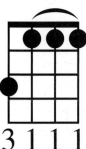
3 2 1 1

B♭
3fr.
1 2 4 3

B♭maj7
3fr.
1 3 3 3

B♭6
3fr.
1 3 1 4

B♭m
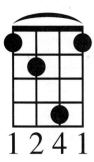
3 1 1 1

B♭m
3fr.
1 3 4 2

B♭m7
1 1 1 1

B♭m6
2 1 3 1

B♭7
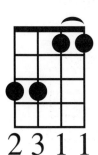
1 2 4 1

B♭7
3fr.
1 3 2 4

B♭9
1 2 1 3

B♭13
1 2 3 4

B♭sus
2 3 1 1

B♭7sus
1 3 4 1

B♭dim7
1 3 2 4

B♭+
4 3 2 1

*B♭ and A♯ are two names for the same note.

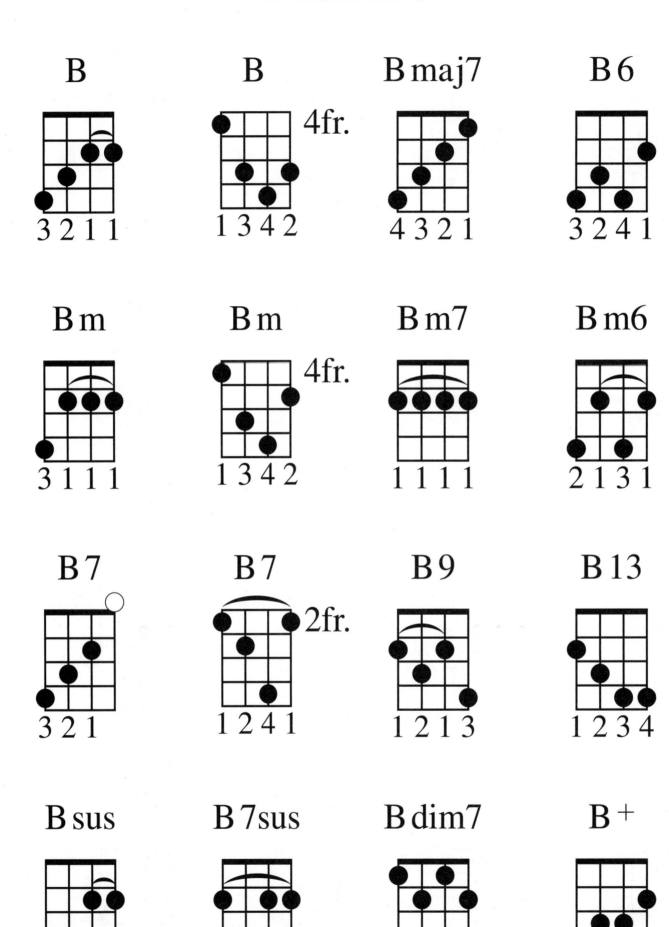

C CHORDS

C
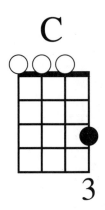
3

C
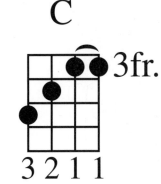
3fr.
3 2 1 1

Cmaj7
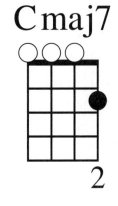
2

C6
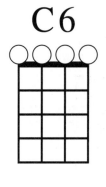

Cm
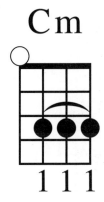
1 1 1

Cm
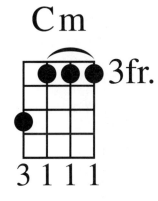
3fr.
3 1 1 1

Cm7
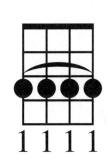
1 1 1 1

Cm6
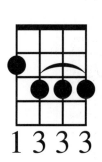
1 3 3 3

C7
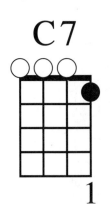
1

C7
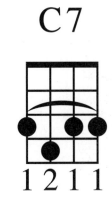
1 2 1 1

C9
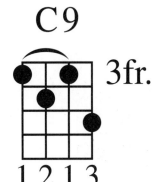
3fr.
1 2 1 3

C13
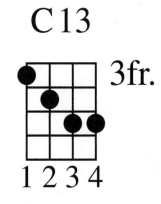
3fr.
1 2 3 4

Csus
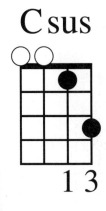
1 3

C7sus
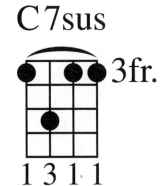
3fr.
1 3 1 1

Cdim7
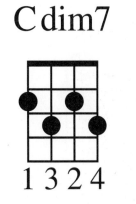
1 3 2 4

C+
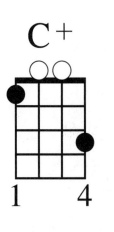
1 4

C♯ (D♭) CHORDS*

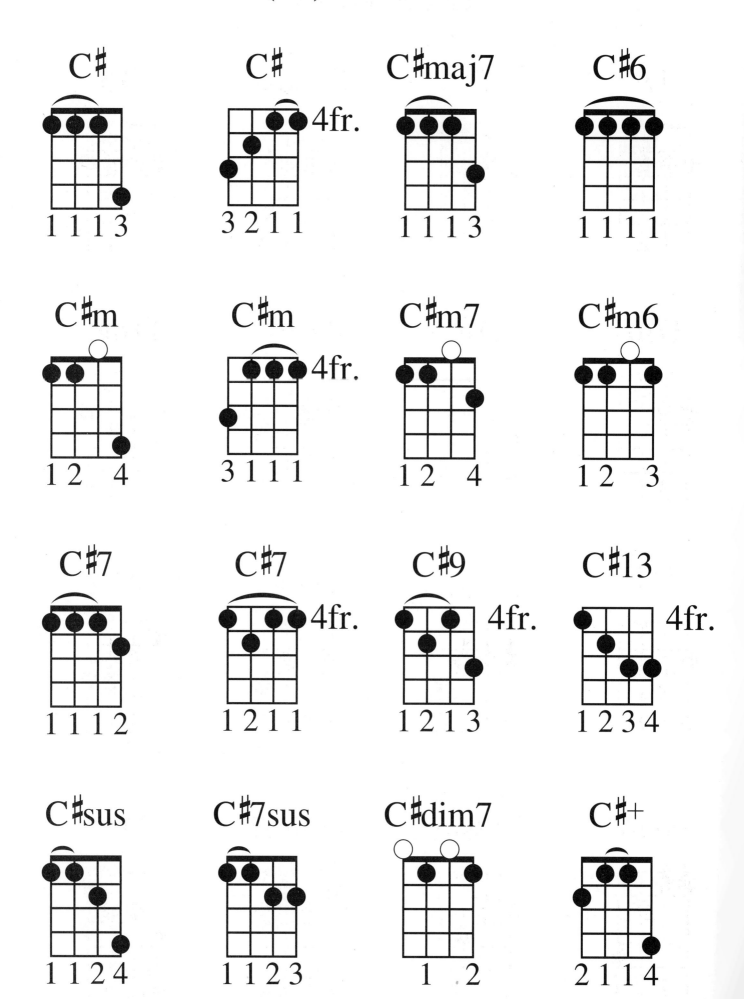

*C♯ and D♭ are two names for the same note.

D CHORDS

D
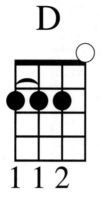
1 1 2

D
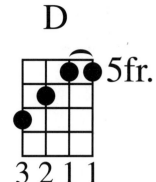
3 2 1 1   5fr.

Dmaj7
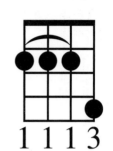
1 1 1 3

D6
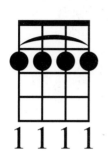
1 1 1 1

Dm
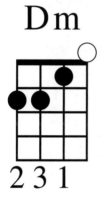
2 3 1

Dm
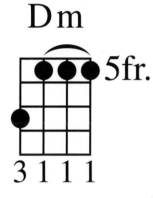
3 1 1 1   5fr.

Dm7
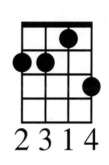
2 3 1 4

Dm6

2 3 1 4

D7
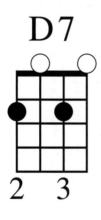
2   3

D7
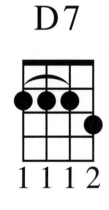
1 1 1 2

D9
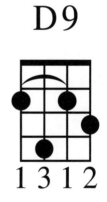
1 3 1 2

D13
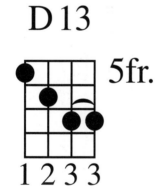
1 2 3 3   5fr.

Dsus
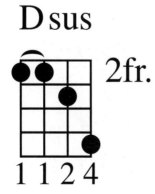
1 1 2 4   2fr.

D7sus
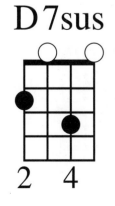
2   4

Ddim7
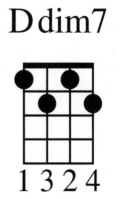
1 3 2 4

D+
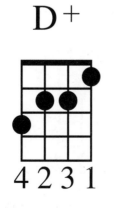
4 2 3 1

E♭ (D♯) CHORDS*

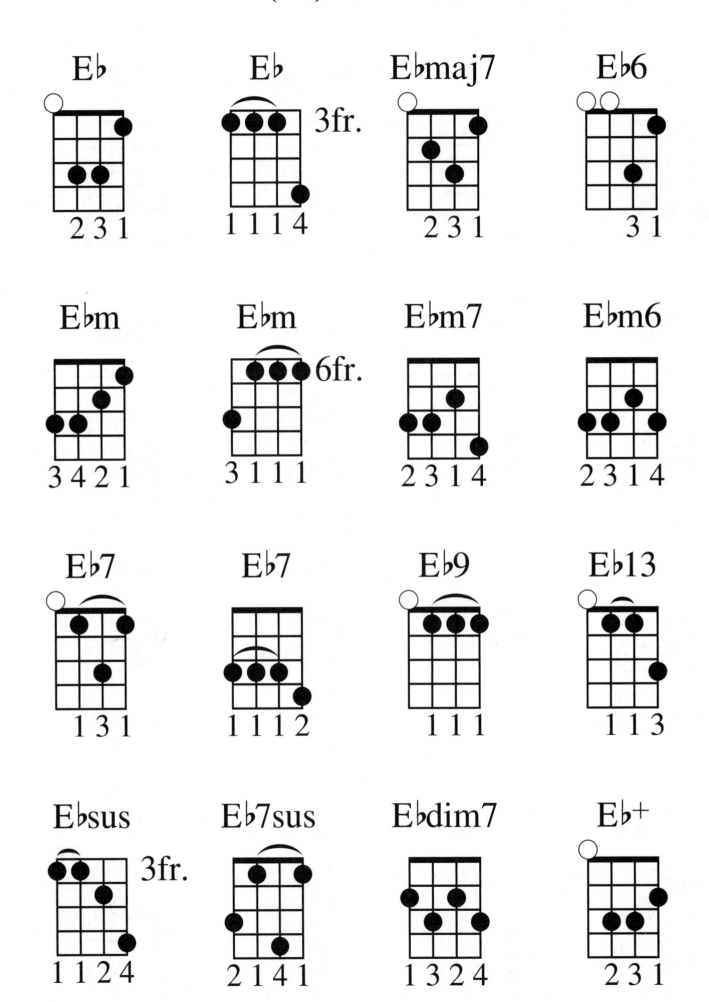

*E♭ and D♯ are two names for the same note.

E CHORDS

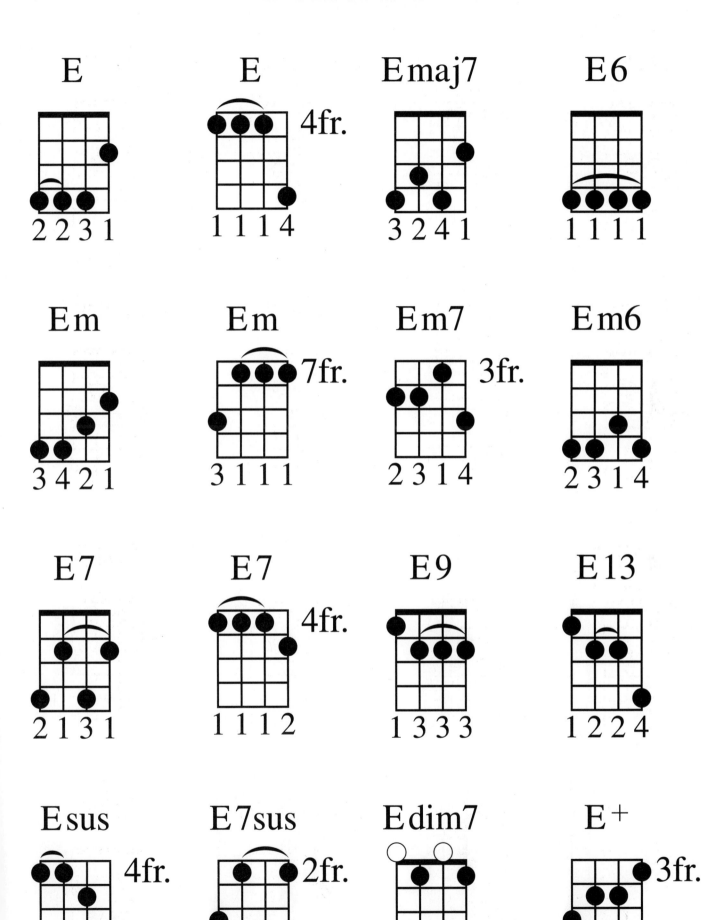

F CHORDS

F
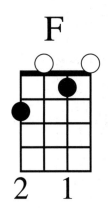

2   1

F
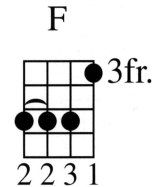
3fr.

2 2 3 1

Fmaj7
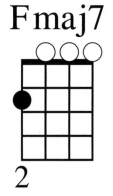

2

F6
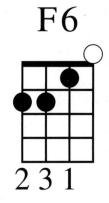

2 3 1

Fm
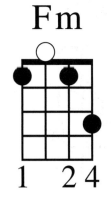

1   2 4

Fm
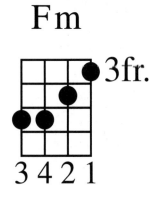
3fr.

3 4 2 1

Fm7
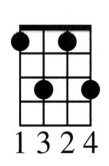

1 3 2 4

Fm6
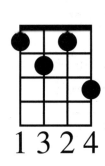

1 3 2 4

F7
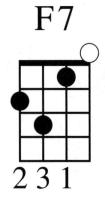

2 3 1

F7
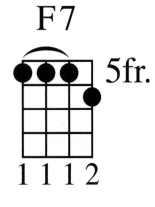
5fr.

1 1 1 2

F9
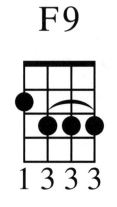

1 3 3 3

F13
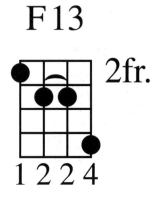
2fr.

1 2 2 4

Fsus
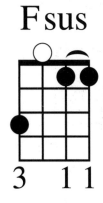

3   1 1

F7sus
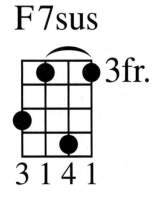
3fr.

3 1 4 1

Fdim7
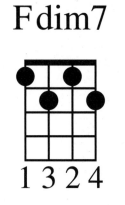

1 3 2 4

F+
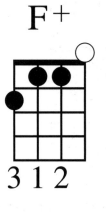

3 1 2

F♯ (G♭) CHORDS*

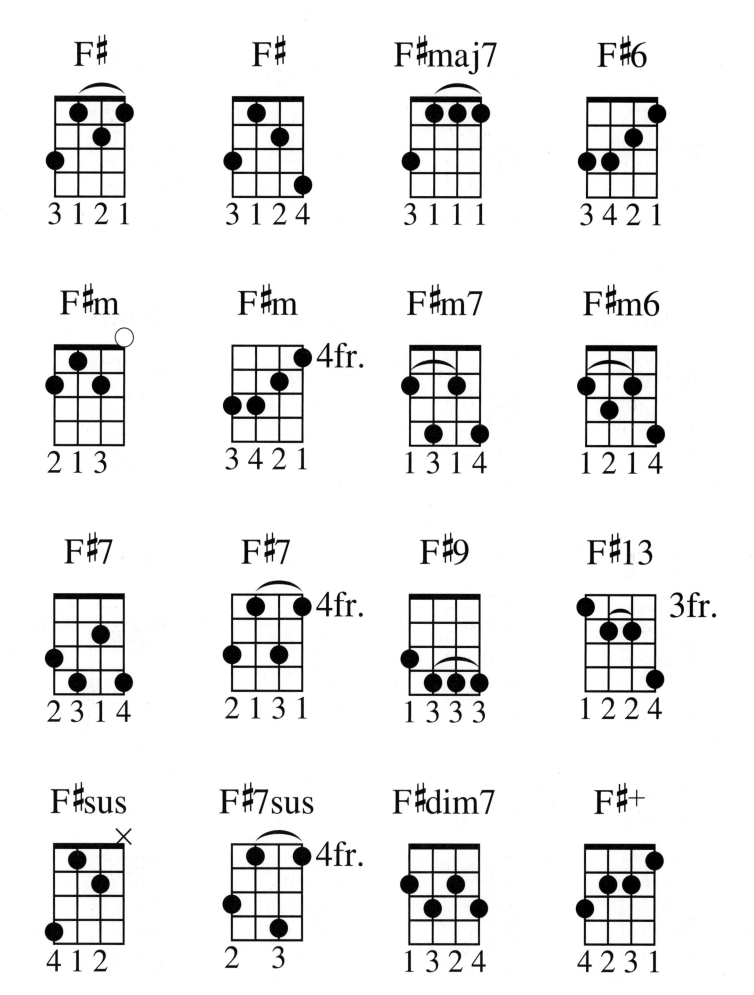

*F♯ and G♭ are two names for the same note.

G CHORDS

G
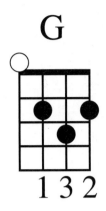
1 3 2

G
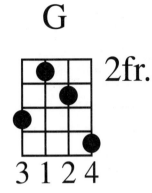
2fr.
3 1 2 4

Gmaj7
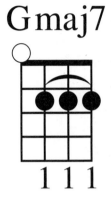
1 1 1

G6
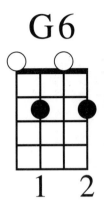
1   2

Gm
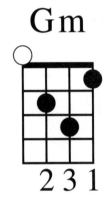
2 3 1

Gm
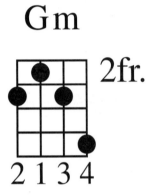
2fr.
2 1 3 4

Gm7
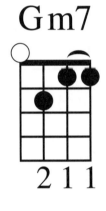
2 1 1

Gm6
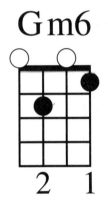
2   1

G7
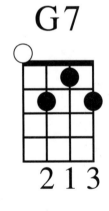
2 1 3

G7
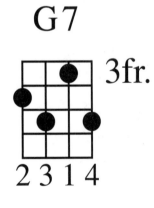
3fr.
2 3 1 4

G9
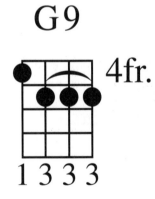
4fr.
1 3 3 3

G13
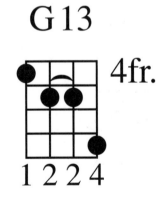
4fr.
1 2 2 4

Gsus
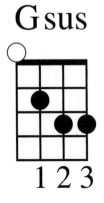
1 2 3

G7sus
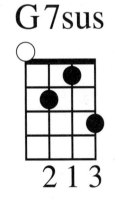
2 1 3

Gdim7
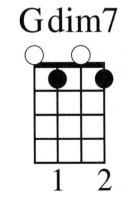
1   2

G+
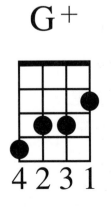
4 2 3 1

A♭ (G♯) CHORDS

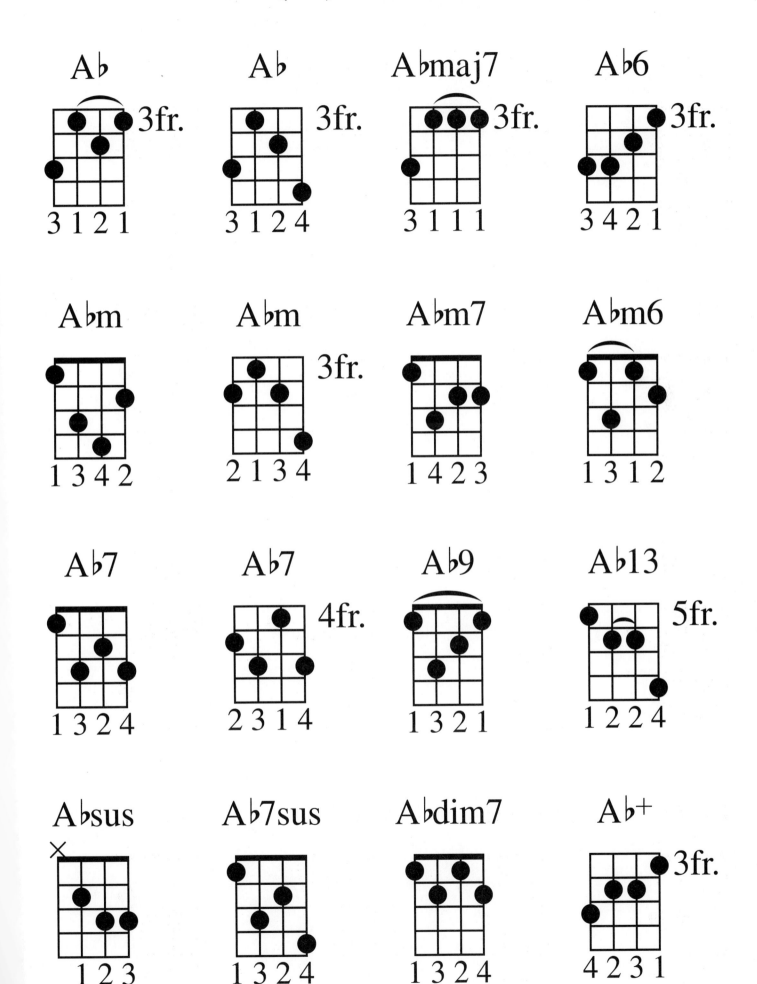

*A♭ and G♯ are two names for the same note.

TABLATURE EXPLANATION

TAB illustrates the four strings of the ukulele.
Notes and chords are indicated by the placement of fret numbers on each string.

Standard ukulele tuning for soprano, concert, and tenor models is G–C–E–A with the fourth string tuned a whole step lower than the open 1st string.

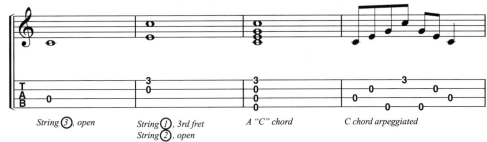

String ③, open   *String ①, 3rd fret*   *A "C" chord*   *C chord arpeggiated*
                          String ②, open

Alternate Tuning:
Some players (including Israel "Iz" Kamakawiwoʻole) tune their fourth string down one octave from standard ukulele (similar to the first four strings of a guitar with a capo on the 5th fret).

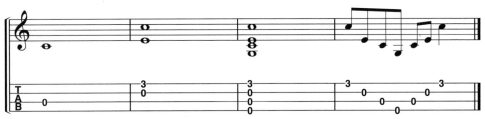

ARTICULATIONS

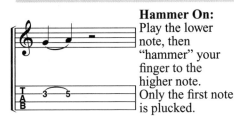

Hammer On:
Play the lower note, then "hammer" your finger to the higher note. Only the first note is plucked.

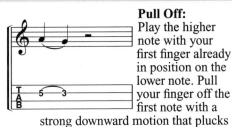

Pull Off:
Play the higher note with your first finger already in position on the lower note. Pull your finger off the first note with a strong downward motion that plucks the string—sounding the lower note.

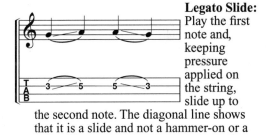

Legato Slide:
Play the first note and, keeping pressure applied on the string, slide up to the second note. The diagonal line shows that it is a slide and not a hammer-on or a pull-off.

Palm Mute:
The notes are muted (muffled) by placing the palm of the pick hand lightly on the strings, just in front of the bridge.

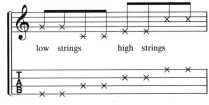

Muted Strings:
A percussive sound is produced by striking the strings while laying the fret hand across them.

HARMONICS

Natural Harmonic:
A finger of the fret hand lightly touches the string at the note indicated in the TAB and is plucked by the pick producing a bell-like sound called a harmonic.

RHYTHM SLASHES

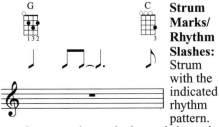

Strum Marks/ Rhythm Slashes:
Strum with the indicated rhythm pattern. Strum marks can be located above the staff or within the staff.

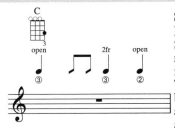

Single Notes with Rhythm Slashes:
Sometimes single notes are incorporated into a strum pattern. The circled number below is the string and the fret number is above.

PICK DIRECTION

Downstrokes and Upstrokes:
The downstroke is indicated with this symbol ⊓ and the upstroke is indicated with this ∨.

BENDING NOTES

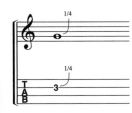

Slight Bend/ Quarter-Tone Bend:
Play the note and bend string sharp.

Half Step:
Play the note and bend string one half step (one fret).